MARRIAGE ON THE ROCK

———

DISCUSSION GUIDE

The first several years of mine and Karen's marriage could be best described as two parched people trying to satisfy their thirsts in a desert. As most couples do, we married one another because we each believed the other could meet our needs and fulfill our desires. Our courtship had not been perfect, yet we believed that any problems we experienced could be solved if only we were married. So, we jumped from the proverbial frying pan into the fire and tied the knot.

As a result of poor premarital preparation, after several years of collective ignorance and immaturity, we found ourselves "out of love." Every year, we had fought with increasing frequency and intensity, becoming more emotionally numb and disillusioned with each quarrel. However, the darkest moments began when we both became convinced we had made a mistake. If only we had chosen the right persons to marry, we would not have all of these problems—or so we thought.

Marriage on the Rock is the result of what God has shown Karen and me about marriage. In this spiritual-education process, God healed our marriage and gave us a love for one another far beyond any we had ever known or imagined. Today, after more than forty-five years of marriage, not only are we deeply in love, but we also understand how to stay in love. We have learned how to meet one another's needs as we walk through life's seasons and challenges.

When couples understand and apply God's foundations of marriage to their relationship, they are transformed. I hope this study is a blessing to you wherever you are on your marriage journey. I pray it encourages you and brings hope to your marriage.

Blessings,

Jimmy Evans

HOW TO USE THIS DISCUSSION GUIDE

1. **The Discussion Guide** Read through each session together as a couple or with your group. The verses and key thoughts are great take-aways to meditate on.
2. **Watch the XO Now Online Videos** Jimmy Evans provides a short time of teaching for each session. Watch the video that corresponds with your session.
3. **Questions & Activation** Work through some of the questions with your spouse and/or group. Then set aside a time to do the "Just You And Me" part together as a couple.

HOW TO WATCH THE XO NOW ONLINE VIDEOS

1. This discussion guide comes with **One Free Month of XO Now!** Go to **xomarriage.com/now** and enter the coupon code: **LASTINGLOVE** during checkout.
2. Log into your XO Now account and search 'Marriage on The Rock' to find *Marriage on The Rock* videos.

*If you already have an XO Now account you can still use the Free Month off coupon by going to xomarriage.com/now/myaccount, clicking Edit Subscription, then Apply coupon, entering the coupon code and clicking update subscription. The discount will be applied to your next invoice.

**This coupon only works if you sign up through our website. It will not work if you try to sign up through the apps (Apple, Google, Roku, Amazon) or if you have previously signed up through the apps.

CONTENTS

THE MOST IMPORTANT ISSUE IN MARRIAGE

"Whoever drinks of this water will thirst again, but whoever drinks of the water that I shall give him will never thirst. But the water that I shall give him will become in him a fountain of water springing up into everlasting life."

GENESIS 2:24–25 (NKJV)

The most important issue in marriage is a personal relationship with God. He meets our deepest needs for acceptance, identity, security and purpose. If we don't allow God to meet those needs, we will seek a person to do it—and we will be disappointed. When we experience an unfulfilling marriage, it's because we are wanting a husband or wife to address needs only God can meet. For marriage to be successful, we must base our marriage on God and His Word.

The love of God heals our hurts and gives us confidence for successful relationships. Allowing God into your marriage will transform the way you see yourself and your spouse.

"For the sake of your life and the lives of those around you, trust Jesus to meet your needs. Only a person who trusts in Jesus to this depth can truly have a successful marriage." — Jimmy Evans, *Marriage on the Rock* | Pg. 10

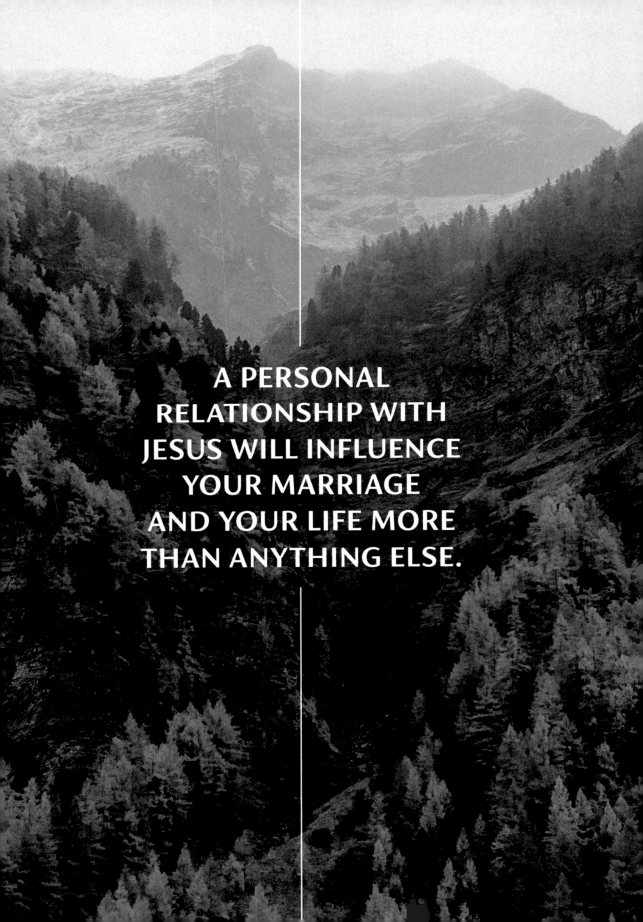

A PERSONAL RELATIONSHIP WITH JESUS WILL INFLUENCE YOUR MARRIAGE AND YOUR LIFE MORE THAN ANYTHING ELSE.

Watch "Session 1 – The Most Important Issue in Marriage" on XO Now.

DISCUSSION QUESTIONS

1. Have you ever felt that God was angry about your failures or sin? How does it feel to know He loves you just the way you are?

2. Do you depend daily on God to meet your four basic needs?

3. What does acceptance mean to you? How does a relationship with God fill that need?

4. Jimmy says identity is a basic human need. How would you describe your identity? Who are you?

5. How does marriage make you feel secure?

6. What would you consider your purpose in life? Are you and your spouse on the same page?

JUST YOU AND ME

Share with your spouse about the time when you accepted God's gift of a relationship with Jesus Christ. Do you have a dependent daily relationship with Him? If not, pray with your spouse and give your heart to God. Let your group leader or pastor know about this too!

THE LAWS OF PRIORITY AND PURSUIT

"Therefore a man shall leave his father and mother and be joined to his wife, and they shall become one flesh. And they were both naked, the man and his wife, and were not ashamed."

GENESIS 2:24-25 (NKJV)

When God created marriage, He created it upon the laws of His Word. One of those is the Law of Priority. Marriage only works when we put it first. There are two steps to establishing and maintaining the right priorities in marriage. First, priority has to be proven in real terms, through sacrifice, time, energy and attitude. We also must protect our priorities, because most marriages are destroyed by good things (work and kids, for example) that are out of priority.

The second law of marriage is the Law of Pursuit. One of the biggest misconceptions about marriage is that marriage is easy if you marry the right person. That's untrue, because every marriage takes work. When you fall in love, you put great effort into the relationship. To stay in love, you have to put in the same daily energy. Love is a perishable commodity: it has to be renewed day after day.

"Unfortunately, misunderstanding and underestimating the importance of these Scriptures has left couples throughout the ages needlessly groping for solid truth about marriage, when that truth has been right under their noses." — Jimmy Evans, *Marriage on the Rock* | Pg. 17

WHEN GOD CREATES
ANYTHING, HE CREATES
IT FOR SUCCESS. WE WERE
MADE FOR MARRIAGE, AND
HAVE A 100 PERCENT CHANCE
OF SUCCESS IN MARRIAGE IF
WE DO IT GOD'S WAY.

Watch "Session 2 - The Laws of Priority and Pursuit" on XO Now.

DISCUSSION QUESTIONS

1. What do you think about the idea of "legitimate jealousy" in marriage?

2. What good things can become problems when they take improper priority?

3. What's one way you or your spouse have sacrificed in your marriage?

4. Describe what you think it means to put effort or energy into marriage.

5. What does the concept of agape love—love by choice—look like in your relationship?

6. How are you and your spouse different? How do you choose to love each other consistently despite your differences?

JUST YOU AND ME

Talk to your spouse about a time when violating the Law of Priority or the Law of Pursuit caused problems in your marriage. Tell your spouse something they can do to serve you this week and then both of you make the effort to serve each other in that way.

THE LAWS OF POSSESSION AND PURITY

"The husband should fulfill his marital duty to his wife, and likewise the wife to her husband. The wife does not have authority over her own body but yields it to her husband. In the same way, the husband does not have authority over his own body but yields it to his wife."

1 CORINTHIANS 7:3-4 (NIV)

God created marriage to succeed when we follow the four laws of marriage. After Priority and Pursuit, the third law of marriage is the Law of Possession. God created marriage to share everything. That's what it means to "become one flesh." If we go into a marriage without giving our spouse full ownership over everything in our lives—from children to money—it creates problems. We violate the Law of Possession through dominance, independence, and personal protection.

The fourth law of marriage is the Law of Purity. Eden means "pleasure and delight" and God created men and women to be naked and unashamed. When you are living in purity, you can expose your most sensitive areas to your spouse without problems. But when sin enters, you stop trusting each other and hide your differences and sensitivities. From our most vulnerable emotions to our most personal dreams, we must be each other's safe places.

"The words 'mine' and 'yours' are fine when you are single. However, when you marry, you must get a new vocabulary." — Jimmy Evans, *Marriage on the Rock* | Pg. 53

MARRIAGE IS DESIGNED BY GOD TO BE A TOTAL SHARING OF LIFE BETWEEN TWO PEOPLE. IT SHOULD ALSO BE A PLACE FOR MENTAL, EMOTIONAL, SPIRITUAL, AND PHYSICAL TRANSPARENCY.

Watch "Session 3 - The Laws of Possession and Purity" on XO Now.

DISCUSSION QUESTIONS

1. Were there any aspects of your pre-marriage life that were hard to surrender when you got married? Are there still areas of your life that have been hard to surrender? If so, what are they?

2. What are some things that can cause problems if you don't give full ownership to your spouse? Do you have an example of this in your own marriage?

3. What does it mean to be "naked and unashamed" in your marriage?

4. How would your marriage benefit from more vulnerability?

5. In what ways do you rely on your spouse to be a "safe place"?

JUST YOU AND ME

Examine your own life. Is there something you are holding back? Are there any places where you need to restore trust with your spouse? Share this with your spouse and allow them to ask questions about how to grow in trust and transparency.

A MAN'S NEEDS

"Wives, submit to your husbands as to the Lord."

EPHESIANS 5:22 (NKJV)

One of the greatest contributors to failed marriages is selfishness. A phenomenal marriage is made of two servants who are in love and committed to meeting each other's needs. That's why it is important for a wife to know her husband's needs and understand how to address them.

Men's greatest need is honor and respect. Men and women are equals, but men gravitate to the place where they are honored. They need respect and the first place they find it should be their spouse. Men also have other important needs: the need for sex, the need for friendship, and the need for support at home. A dream marriage begins when each spouse serves the other sacrificially.

"As you serve, God will honor and bless you. As you lay your life down for your mate, you will find the life you have been seeking." — Jimmy Evans, *Marriage on the Rock* | Pg. 79

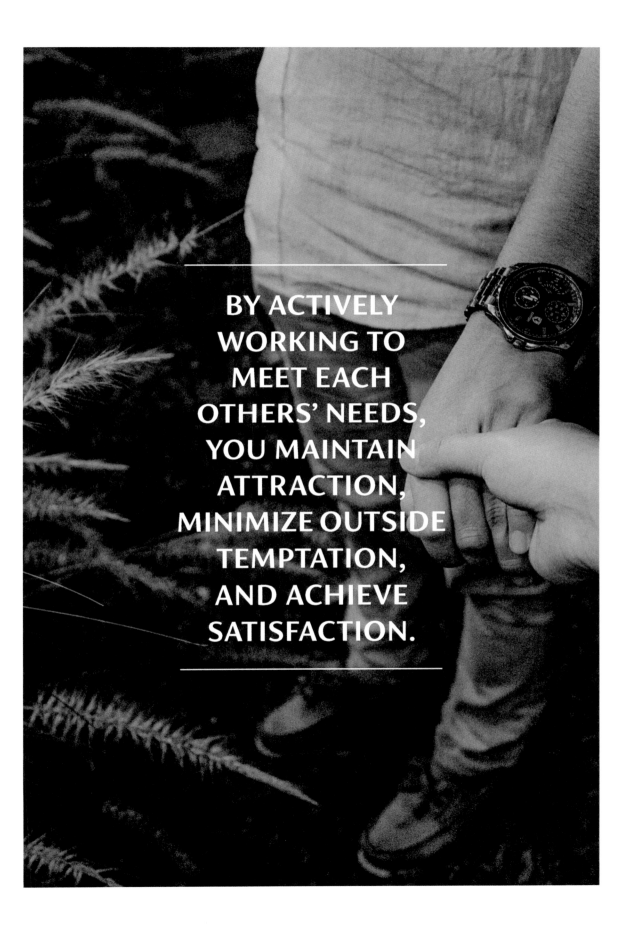

BY ACTIVELY WORKING TO MEET EACH OTHERS' NEEDS, YOU MAINTAIN ATTRACTION, MINIMIZE OUTSIDE TEMPTATION, AND ACHIEVE SATISFACTION.

Watch "Session 4 – A Man's Needs" on XO Now.

DISCUSSION QUESTIONS

1. The passage in Ephesians presents biblical roles for men and women. How do these roles differ from how our culture views relationships?

2. Jimmy says, "If we could meet our own needs, we wouldn't get married." Do you agree?

3. Men, what does respect mean to you in the context of marriage?

4. Women, what does it mean to honor our husbands where we want them to be (not where they are)?

5. Statistically, most men are more sexual than their wives. Is this true in your marriage?

6. Friendship is a major need for men. What does friendship look like in your relationship?

JUST YOU AND ME

Focus on building friendship between you and your spouse. Wives, ask your husband what he wants to do for a fun night out and then go do it. Remind each other why you like being married. Have sex and enjoy being together!

A WOMAN'S NEEDS

"Husbands, love your wives, just as Christ also loved the church and gave Himself for her..."

EPHESIANS 5:25 (NKJV)

In the same way it's important for a woman to understand her husband's needs and work to meet them, it is also crucial for a man to understand his wife's needs. The biblical standard for a husband is to give his life for his wife. He should love her more than he loves himself and be willing to sacrifice for her.

A woman's greatest need is for security. Women feel most secure in a marriage to a sacrificial, sensitive man. They feel insecure married to a selfish, detached man. Women also need non-sexual affection, open and honest communication, and leadership. They don't want to be dominated, but they do want their husbands to lovingly initiate conversations about the children, romance, finances and spiritual matters. While only Jesus meets our deepest needs, God has designed marriage so that we meet specific needs in each other's lives.

"Biblical roles keep a relationship growing year after year. When you don't think it can get any better—it does." — Jimmy Evans, *Marriage on the Rock* | Pg. 78

XO ▶ Watch "Session 5 - A Woman's Needs" on XO Now.

DISCUSSION QUESTIONS

1. Why do you think a man with a sacrificial mindset is so attractive to women?

2. Male or female, what does romance communicate to you?

3. What is non-sexual affection to you? Are the two of you on the same page regarding affection?

4. Do the two of you communicate differently? How do you overcome these differences?

5. What do you think about the idea that women should be more sexual than they feel, and men should be more conversational than they feel?

6. What does leadership look like in the context of your marriage?

JUST BETWEEN US

Men, take your wife to dinner and just talk. Ask her questions about her day, talk about your dreams together and what's going on in your life right now. Receive bonus points if you go see a movie afterwards that will make you cry.

THE POWER
OF POSITIVE
COMMUNICATION

"Death and life are in the power of the tongue..."

PROVERBS 18:21 (NKJV)

Communication is how we get to know each other, fall in love with each other, and become one. There are two common problems related to communication in marriage. The first is not understanding the immense power of words. Words are lasting and they reveal the condition of our hearts. Just as a tree is known by its fruit, a heart is known by its words.

The second problem is when a couple doesn't understand the communication differences between men and women. Men are emotionally modest and women are emotionally immodest. Communication is as important to women as sex is to men. Husbands need to respect their wives' need for patient, honest, emotional communication. There are five standards of successful communication in marriage: caring, praise, truth, faith, and surrender.

"Words possess incredible power—power to wound or heal, to destroy or build up." — Jimmy Evans, *Marriage on the Rock* | Pg. 216

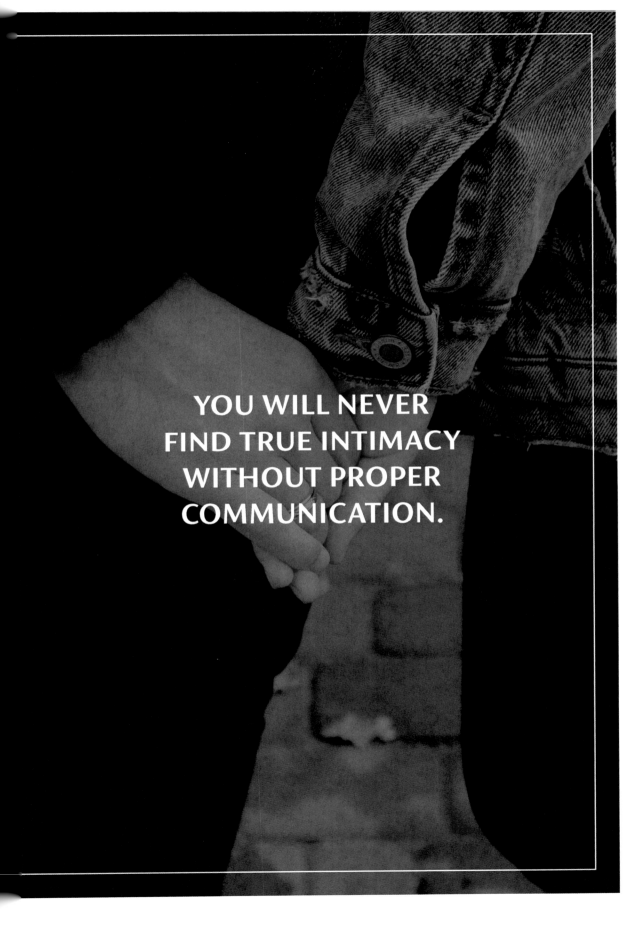

YOU WILL NEVER
FIND TRUE INTIMACY
WITHOUT PROPER
COMMUNICATION.

Watch "Session 6 – The Power of Positive Communication" on XO Now.

DISCUSSION QUESTIONS

1. Who is more likely to initiate conversation in your marriage?

2. What are some ways to add more positive words to your marriage?

3. How are the two of you different when it comes to communication?

4. How often do the two of you just sit down with each other and talk? How many minutes a day do you think you spend in one-on-one communication?

5. What is one positive, encouraging thing you particularly love to hear your spouse say to you?

JUST YOU AND ME

Commit to talking at least one hour per week with no interruptions. Schedule it if you need to. Sit down this week and honestly share with your spouse what areas of communication you need most right now. Both of you share how you can grow in these areas.

FINANCIAL SUCCESS IN MARRIAGE

"Can two walk together, unless they are agreed?"

AMOS 3:3 (NKJV)

Marriage is the number-one wealth-producing entity on earth. At the same time, financial problems are the top reason people divorce. Money can bring tremendous blessings or tremendous stress. To have financial success in marriage, there are five traps to avoid.

The first is not making Jesus Lord of your finances. When Jesus is Lord, He blesses. The second is disrespecting your spouse's financial perspective and input, especially since we have different money languages. The third is giving one spouse disproportionate control over the finances. The fourth danger is chronic disagreement about financial decisions, priorities, and values. The fifth trap is debt—especially credit card debt. Avoid these hurdles—give Jesus control and money will be a blessing rather than a source of problems in your marriage.

"Regardless of your financial situation, you need to respect the powerful influence finances have on your marriage." — Jimmy Evans, *Marriage on the Rock* | Pg. 230

—

UNLESS YOU TRUST JESUS WITH YOUR FINANCES, MONEY WILL CAUSE FIGHTING AND INSECURITY.

—

XO ▶ Watch "Session 7 – Financial Success in Marriage" on XO Now.

DISCUSSION QUESTIONS

1. Do you know anyone who has plenty of material blessings but seems miserable—or vice versa?

2. Describe a time in your life when God has answered a prayer related to your finances.

3. How do you and your spouse share or divide up financial responsibilities in your marriage?

4. Do the two of you have any personal rules or feelings about debt?

5. Have you talked as a couple about the ultimate purpose of your finances? If so, what is it?

6. What shared values do you have with your spouse in regards to your money?

JUST YOU AND ME

Take the time to revisit your budget. If you don't have one, make one! Talk to your spouse about your perspective on money. How are the two of you alike? How are you different? Ask God to guide your decision-making. In prayer, if you haven't already, give your money and financial life to Jesus.

SEXUAL FULFILLMENT IN MARRIAGE

"And they were both naked, the man and his wife, and were not ashamed."

GENESIS 2:25 (NKJV)

Sex makes marriage better. When you're having good sex, it enhances the relationship. But bad sex reveals other problems—like poor communication, stress, or anger. God created sex for pleasure and lifelong enjoyment in marriage, but placed parameters around sex for our protection. God gave men and women sexual differences in order to make relationships more fulfilling and dynamic.

There are five ingredients to sexual fulfillment in marriage. First, commit to meeting your spouse's sexual needs in a faithful manner. Second, communicate your sexual needs to one another. Third, commit to sexual purity to protect your marriage. Fourth, be honest and accountable about sexual temptations. Finally, refuse to be close friends with people who are violating the marriage covenant.

"God is not a prude, and sex is not dirty. It is a wonderful creation designed to give us pleasure." — Jimmy Evans, *Marriage on the Rock* | Pg. 255

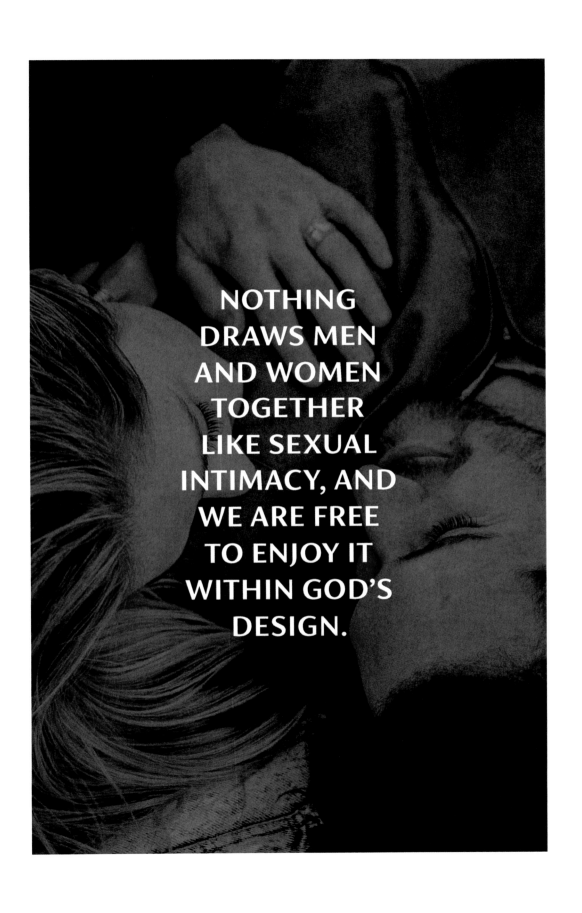

NOTHING DRAWS MEN AND WOMEN TOGETHER LIKE SEXUAL INTIMACY, AND WE ARE FREE TO ENJOY IT WITHIN GOD'S DESIGN.

Watch "Session 8 – Sexual Fulfillment in Marriage" on XO Now.

DISCUSSION QUESTIONS

1. Have you ever struggled to see sex as something God created for your pleasure?

2. What gets in the way of your sex life? (Ex. kids, time, energy) What can you do to limit those distractions?

3. Do you agree that "for men, sex stimulates our emotions" and "with women, emotions stimulate sex"? Why or why not?

4. Do you and your spouse have each other's internet passwords?

5. Have the two of you ever considered scheduling sex within your marriage?

6. How often do you and your spouse set aside a date night together?

JUST BETWEEN US

Talk about sex while on a lunch date. Each of you communicate your needs and expectations. Talk about what you like and don't like. Then, make changes if necessary!

DESTRUCTIVE HUSBANDS AND WIVES

"My people are destroyed for lack of knowledge."

HOSEA 4:6 (NKJV)

Chronically unhappy marriages occur because one or more spouses exhibit destructive behavior. People become destructive for four reasons: simple ignorance about how to have a successful marriage, past hurts that haven't been dealt with, bad friends and negative influences, and defensiveness.

These result in four primary destructive behaviors in marriage. The first is criticism. The second is control and dominance. The third is emotional abandonment. The fourth is cruelty and abuse. If any of these destructive behaviors are present in your marriage, submit that part of your life to the Lord. If you need to get help in order to change your behavior, don't hesitate to do so.

"I was a destructive husband myself. But if not for the grace of God, I would either still be destroying our marriage or, even more probably, be divorced." — Jimmy Evans, *Marriage on the Rock* | Pg. 86

MANY OF US ENTER
MARRIAGE WITH
DESTRUCTIVE
TENDENCIES. WHEN
OUR BEHAVIOR IS
DESTRUCTIVE, THE
ONLY ANSWER IS
TO IDENTIFY IT AND
CORRECT IT.

XO ▶ Watch "Session 9 – Destructive Husbands and Wives" on XO Now.

DISCUSSION QUESTIONS

1. Going in, do you feel you were prepared at all for marriage?

2. Have you and your spouse ever read a marriage book together? What was it and what did you learn from it?

3. Have you seen your friends have a positive or negative effect on your relationship or someone else's?

4. What would your marriage look like if you followed the 10-to-1 rule of 10 positive statements for every negative one?

5. Were you raised in a home where one parent was clearly dominant over the other parent? How did that affect you and your family?

JUST YOU AND ME

Share with your spouse one area where you feel you might be showing destructive behavior. What can you do to move past those tendencies?

RAISING CHILDREN AS YOU BUILD A GREAT MARRIAGE

"Train up a child in the way he should go, and when he is old he will not depart from it."

PROVERBS 22:6 (NKJV)

We all want to raise great kids—but not at the expense of marriage. Three simple principles can ensure your children and marriage are both successful and healthy. First, marriage precedes children in priority. Raising children is a temporary assignment, but marriage is for a lifetime.

Secondly, you and your spouse have to be unified. You should always honor each other in front of your children and make your children honor your spouse. Make sure you show affection and enforce discipline without significant differences. Third, parenting takes faith that your children will learn by watching you do the right thing.

"When we fail to love our children and to meet their needs properly, they can become major problems and a threat to our marriages."
— Jimmy Evans, *Marriage on the Rock* | Pg. 240

RAISE GREAT CHILDREN BY PRIORITIZING YOUR MARRIAGE AND MAKING THE WORD OF GOD THE FOUNDATION OF YOUR FAMILY.

XO ▶ Watch "Session 10 – Raising Children as You Build a Great Marriage" on XO Now.

DISCUSSION QUESTIONS

1. How does building a strong marriage enable you to be good parents?

2. The illustration about putting your airplane oxygen mask on before your kids is memorable. What might that look like in "real life"?

3. Do you agree that children can pick up on tension between you and your spouse—even if you're not fighting in front of them?

4. Based on your example, what is one thing you hope your kids learn by watching your marriage?

5. What are some of the important traditions you're protecting in your marriage?

JUST YOU AND ME

Talk with each other about what your marriage will look like after your children leave home. What steps do you need to take now to create that dream?

PARENTS, PAST AND PRESENT

"...visiting the iniquity of the fathers upon the children and the children's children to the third and the fourth generation."

EXODUS 34:7 (NKJV)

Parents and in-laws are a blessing, but if not handled properly, these relationships can cause problems. Iniquities and inner vows result from imperfect parenting. Certain sins run in families, and the word iniquity means being "bent" in a certain direction—toward a sin like chauvinism, racism, or substance abuse.

Inner vows are self-comforting promises we make to ourselves in response to difficulty or pain. (For instance, "I'll never treat my children like that.") When you make yourself a promise, you put yourself in the position of God. That promise or "inner vow" prevents Jesus from being Lord over that part of your life. Inner vows prohibit growth and make you unteachable. To break an iniquity or inner vow, you have to recognize it, take responsibility for your behavior, repent of the sin, forgive those who hurt you, and make Jesus Lord over those parts of your life.

We are instructed to honor our parents, but we must also set boundaries with them. This includes protecting a spouse from the meddling of in-laws.

"Parenting is more caught than taught. In other words, children are much more influenced by who we are and what we do than by what we say or teach." — Jimmy Evans, *Marriage on the Rock* | Pg. 242

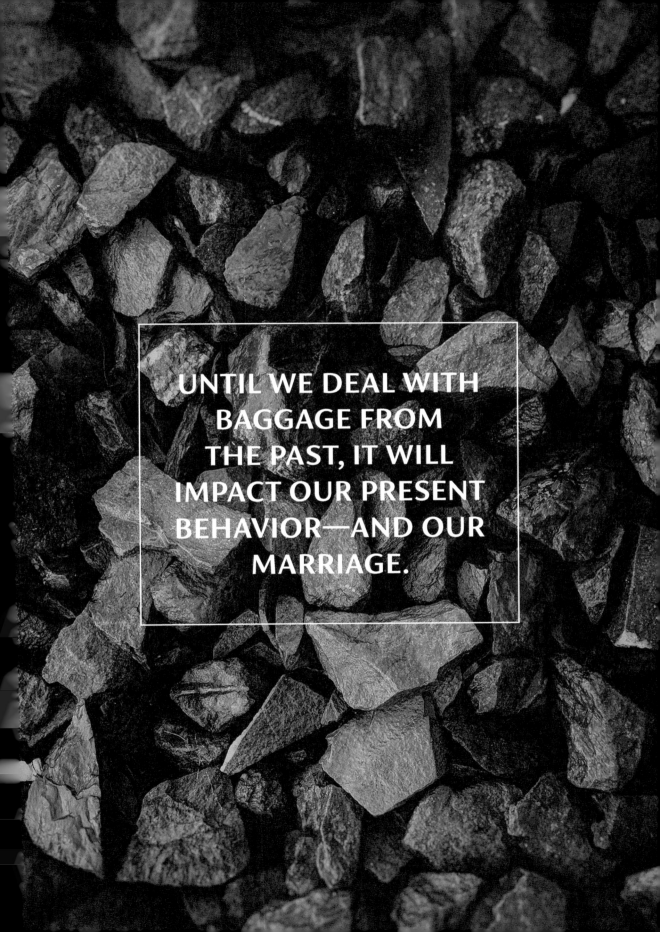

UNTIL WE DEAL WITH
BAGGAGE FROM
THE PAST, IT WILL
IMPACT OUR PRESENT
BEHAVIOR—AND OUR
MARRIAGE.

XO ▶ Watch "Session 11 – Parents, Past and Present" on XO Now.

DISCUSSION QUESTIONS

1. Can you identify any iniquities that may have run in your family?

2. Did the circumstances of your upbringing cause you to make any inner vows? Can you see how that vow may be quietly governing your life?

3. When you got married, was it hard for you to separate from your parents? Why or why not?

4. If parenting is "more caught than taught," what are your children learning about marriage by watching your relationship?

5. Why do you think it's so hard to deal with generational sins or the failures of our parents?

6. What do you think it means to honor our parents as adults?

JUST YOU AND ME

If you have identified an iniquity or inner vow in your life, share it with your spouse. Pray together about it. Ask God to help you repent, forgive, and surrender.

BUILDING SUCCESSFUL BLENDED FAMILIES

"Therefore a man shall leave his father and mother and be joined to his wife, and they shall become one flesh."

GENESIS 2:24 (NKJV)

Many families today are blended families. This occurs when one or both spouses bring children with them from a previous marriage or relationship. The dynamics present in these families result in a higher divorce rate. To ensure success, blended families need to disarm the Day One dynamics of these families.

These dynamics include unresolved feelings toward an ex-spouse, lower trust and higher expectations, inner vows, and the particular challenges of non-biological parenting. In a step-family or blended family, you have to remain focused on keeping God's four laws of marriage: Priority, Possession, Pursuit and Purity. It becomes even more important to make your spouse a priority, trust them, share openly, pursue each other and communicate up-front about kids, ex-spouses and expectations.

"You can succeed if you remarry and blend your families. Indeed, there will be some special challenges. But there are also special rewards for those who dare to meet those challenges." — Jimmy Evans, *Marriage on the Rock* | Pg. 291

TRUST BRINGS INTIMACY, LOVE, CONFIDENCE, AND VULNERABILITY TO A BLENDED FAMILY.

Watch "Session 12 – Building Successful Blended Families" on XO Now.

DISCUSSION QUESTIONS

1. Have you encountered any unexpected emotions or unresolved issues from a past relationship?

2. What do you think of the idea that the devil is the "accuser" of your spouse?

3. Describe a time when you have benefited from forgiving someone. How did it make you feel?

4. If you are in a blended family, what are some of the expectations you brought into marriage? How did you manage them?

5. Why is trust so important in a marriage relationship? What prevents complete trust in a relationship?

6. What does agape love look like within the context of parenting step-children?

JUST YOU AND ME

If you are in a blended marriage, discuss some of the Day One dynamics that were present when you married. Have you and your spouse disarmed them? Which ones do you still need to deal with today?

"If we will obey God's command to prioritize our lives to accommodate and keep our marriages higher than anything except our God, marriage will work wonderfully."

JIMMY EVANS

Made in the USA
Middletown, DE
16 October 2023

40881602R00049